GREEN
WEB

GREEN WEB

POEMS BY

Juan Delgado

The University of Georgia Press

ATHENS AND LONDON

Published by the University of Georgia Press,

Athens, Georgia 30602

©1994 by Juan Delgado

All rights reserved

Designed by Betty Palmer McDaniel

Set in 10/13 Sabon by Tseng Information Systems, Inc.

Printed and bound by Thomson-Shore, Inc.

The paper in this book meets the guidelines for

permanence and durability of the Committee on

Production Guidelines for Book Longevity

of the Council on Library Resources.

Printed in the United States of America

98   97   96   95   94   P   5   4   3   2   1

Library of Congress Cataloging in Publication Data

Delgado, Juan, 1960–

Green web : poems / by Juan Delgado

p.   cm.

ISBN 0-8203-1677-6 (pbk. : alk. paper)

I. Title.

PS3554.E442465G74   1994

811'.54—dc20   94-7789

British Library Cataloging in Publication Data available

FOR MY BEST FRIEND,
My Wife

ACKNOWLEDGMENTS

Grateful acknowledgment is made to the following periodicals in which versions of my poems originally appeared:

Alchemy: "Mad" (as "All Knotted Up"), "The Phone Booth at the Corner"
Connecticut Poetry Review: "Ofelia's Dream" (as "Loosening Braids")
Embers: "Flavio's New Home"
Missouri Review: "The Letters from School" (as "The Pink Letters of Grade School")
Pacific Review: "I Was Not Sure" (as "For Jean")
Penumbra: "Crayons"
Puerto del Sol: "My Mother's Stories"
O!! Zone: "Her Face Floats"

"Flora's Plea to Mary," "Keeping Up," "He Took Her Away" (as "My Father Was Driving Us to America"), "The Letters from School," "Mad," and "Eyes Held by a Landscape" also appeared in my chapbook, *A Change of Worlds.*

CONTENTS

GREEN
WEB

VISITING FATHER

I buzz through two security doors
almost unseen by the guard, busy
scanning a magazine as if he can't read.
Father waits in the recreation room.
A man slaps the back of his neck,
holding it while he rocks his head;
another sweeps the pool table's green
and smiles at me before breaking;
two women talk of paradise, of sons
too young to enter the mental ward.
Others shuffle their slippers around me,
around Father, who watches a TV and pounds
its flickering screen, saving the scene.
Noticing me, he offers the best iced tea
a quarter can pop out, but I go on,
rambling a father-talk only a son
can dish out—how quickly I bore him.
He clicks through the channels and waits
until I give up my big-man act,
but I'm too nervous to stop my chatter,
glancing at the people closing in.

"Hey, follow me," he says, waving me on.
And what a happy lady he leads me to:
Her muumuu drags on the overwaxed floor,
her mirrored orange petals shadowing her.
She sings into a hairbrush, her mike,
then giggles, raising her dress to her knees
and flopping on a chair next to us.
Excited by my staring, she spreads
her legs, digs her hand into her crotch,

I

working herself to half-words and kisses,
waving me closer with her dirty brush,
extending it, wanting me to sing,
but I turn, afraid to look at myself,
embarrassed and scared by her joy.
I leave Father sitting on her lap,
all embraced, walking past a screen
that jumbles voices into waving lines
and for the sake of my father and me,
I begin rehearsing what I will retell.

A MEXICAN FIRE BREATHER

Where the weather is not water
a man sips from a glass jar,
not swallowing the gasoline,
holding in his breath
while holding up his lighter.

In the cloud burst of fire
there are no legions of angels
beyond the air of his lungs,
saints holding the flame of life
on their upturned palms.

In the cloud burst of fire
the man is neither a cross,
fixed while the earth spins,
nor an ancient altar,
raised and tainted with blood.

He is only a man
cleaning your windshield
while you wait at the light.
He peers in your car,
holding in his breath and fire.

SISTERS

At noon we crossed the plaza
so the men would follow our stride:
In front of us the pigeons leaped,
circling in a wave of wings,
long as a royal bride's train.
And you adjusted your skirt
by ironing your thighs
with an evenhanded stroke.

How we labored making our dresses.
With the wax paper cut and pinned,
we traced the patterns with a soap bar
and cut, using only our best scissors,
then basted, always ready to hide
our dresses from Father's watchful eye.

At our father's grocery store
we weighed rice in bags—you shoveled
and I held their mouths open.
We bet cigarettes whose boyfriend
would visit first after Father left.
You always won.

Once our boyfriends drove us
to the country where we picked mangoes.
A farmer yelled from his garden:
"Get away from there. Go away."
We rinsed our sticky hands in the river,
cooling our faces and necks.
Your boyfriend, jokingly, said:
"Be careful of river snakes."
We laughed, throwing sand,
then walked into the tall grass.

4

HE TOOK HER AWAY

Through a car door bound
from swinging open by rope,
Mother saw an oil-soaked road
streaming backwards to Mexico.
Father had broken his promise,
was taking her to America.

And her fingernails took on
the hue of limestone, a yellow
spreading to the wings of moths,
her guayaba tree, a candleholder,
the porcelain hands of a prayer,
fixed in their plea, like hers,
and to her husband's teeth,
rootless and false.

The gravel receded under her,
drawing her in, a wave,
until a flash of sun broke
her trance, and looking back
she glistened, a pillar of salt,
but the yellow line tugged him on.

MERCADO DEL AIRE
(A RADIO SHOW)

For my mother, who brought her songs from Mexico

With her radio she works,
sweeping the crumbs,
then she taps the clock,
stopping its hum.

A man announces a miracle cream
that vanishes warts
and then flips
through a Blue Stamp Book,
describing all the prizes
one can buy.

A mother gets on
begging to know
if her son is still alive.
He was last seen
in Colton, California,
where he did cement work.

A gardener wants to trade
his tools for a ticket
back to Mexico.

With her radio she longs
to see her sister dance
around the rooster
that pecked at her heels.

6

With her radio she sings,
and a lover throws pebbles
at a window and strikes the chord
that announces love.

She cooks,
imagining the plaza
where she walked
past the admiring boys.
She rolls the sticky flour
into a world she longs for.

With her radio the pot boils
and the day dresses her
with its luck.

A JEALOUS FATHER

His lullaby that night is about a man
who seduced Mother with his new car.
The man coaxed her out a window
into the street and drove her away.

The lullaby is about a cornfield
and the thin road they made.
They parked among the rows of corn,
forgetting a signal light ticking yellow,
a yellow flaming the corn silk.

His lullaby is about that cornfield.
When headlights drift into our room,
Father rises and pounds the mattress,
moving with his shadow to the window.

SHE FINDS HER MASK

She finds the devil's grin,
all teeth, Carnival!
A parade of bones
dancing on their way.

KEEPING UP

A country burial. The mourners board
a truck, crowding a small coffin.
The side rails of the truck shake.
A boy leans over the coffin,
seeing the distortion, his face.
He takes in the church's incense
lingering in his aunts' shawls
while they finger their holy beads,
murmur the child's name to Jesus
and bob their heads in devotion.
The dust that trailed them stops,
coiling at the graveyard gates.
They stumble, hip bumping hip,
and his aunts pray and shuffle.
When he helps them off the truck,
he smells their overpolished shoes
and the coffin's newly varnished pine.
In line he walks with that odor,
recalling that the box housing his boots
also smells like an old shoe brush.
Keeping up with the procession,
he wipes his new boots and swats
at the dust rising from his aunts.

TRAPPED

With her straw broom,
Mother pounded the rug
hanging on a clothesline
ready to snap. Bristles
whirled with her swinging,
floating with the morning dust.

I spotted a trapped mouse.
His eyes were black tacks
and his whiskers were frantic
when he dashed around the sink.

I turned on the water.
He could have swum out,
but the water steamed.
His mad leaps kept me
from reaching over him.

With his nose up, he jumped,
wiggling his tail, a lizard.
Only when the hot water hosed him
did he stop squeaking.
The words of my rosary spilled out
like the beads of a broken string.

EARACHE

We walked to the large tent
the religious people had set up.
You, Father, walked ahead
while I counted my steps,
trying to distract myself
from the pain in my ear.
Once we entered the tent,
a woman hugged you, then me,
handing you a song book.
You nudged me through the crowd,
pushing me to the forming line
that led to the stage
where a preacher blessed
people by flicking water at them;
he dipped his fingers into a jar.
I dug my hand into my pocket,
working the lint into a ball.
Scared by the preacher's shouts,
I turned and called for you,
but I could not see you,
find where you had sat.
I felt the pain the most
when I heard myself talk.
I thought about God's voice
and how it must fill
your head until you believe
His voice has become yours.
Ahead of me the preacher
rubbed his hands with water,
as if he were cleaning them,
then reached out and touched

the forehead of a coughing man.
He blessed a woman next,
held her face and whispered,
causing her to cry out.
I simply pointed to my ear.
He tilted my head, the way
a barber does without warning.
The cold water filled my ear,
ran down my cheek and neck,
sharpening my pain.
I noticed the hanging lightbulbs
sway, walking back to you.
I sat in the chair you saved.
Without looking at your face,
I knew you were relieved,
thinking my pain was gone,
so I hid it from you
and sang along with you,
studying the central pole
leading to the tent's mouth
that breathed in the night.
I wished for silence,
for the tent to be His ear.

MRS. LUCY RIVERA

At dusk I fade behind my screen.
A crow picks at a bag, the empty
plastic settles like a fog.

Like my friend, the crow
who sits on a wire like a clothespin,
I squawk at the dying light.

I smear my lipstick, then finger
my bleeding lips, my mascara.
My penciled-in eyebrows are too perfect.

When the young wife sees my face,
she will go on as if nothing is wrong,
both of us pretending.

I listen to sounds no one hears:
a stirring trash can, a leaping cat,
a car with one headlight like a bullet.

I peer through half-closed blinds,
studying the flickering porch lights;
moths flutter like kites without tails.

The people of my street believe
in sleep, in their laboring days.
I linger in my room, and sleep.

HER FACE FLOATS

In the shallow end the beauty
adjusts her bathing cap
and tucks her hair in.
She is a tan penny.

The petals on her cap
blossom with waves.
Her desire fingers the light.
Leisure is her twin sister.

Sun blind, she treads.
Her face floats on her
thousand poses.

A cut shadow swims under her,
clutching at her ankles,
wrestling her body down.

A DAY SPINS

In her mattress his wife sinks,
nursing a bundle wiggling free.
His son curled by his bed rail
tries to kick his nightmare off.
The morning news slaps his porch.
His blinds open, flooding the room.
The stubbornness of his screen door,
the panic of ants in a closing crack
and a whirling car hurry his steps.
In a stiff back reach, he imagines
all the parked cars swinging open,
eager for their drivers' routes,
and a crow's shadow flapping by.
He stands, not denying he casts
that shadow, knowing his day ends
suspended like a toy globe,
and how he longs for his shadow,
for its manta ray wings to scoop
and carry him beyond the roofs
that glitter most in a night rain.

CROW ON A WIRE

In the bathroom
the father rubs a black dye,
the youth of his hair.
From profile to profile,
his eye is a mirror.

Joking how strong he is,
enough to outwork anyone,
he buys his son a drink.
The father's story arranges
empty beer bottles.

Feeling the pool table,
circling the rimming light,
he puffs smoke—he is
a barrel scoping his chances,
the blackness of wings,
lost and surrounded
by his will, his scent.

His purpose is the doing,
the swooping of a crow,
the picking of flesh.

MAD

Dad didn't get picked.
I guess a foreman drove off
with a truck full of workers,
leaving Dad at the curb
waiting all day for the next truck.
Usually he's hired for the day
and too tired to dog everyone.
Now he pounds the table
because he's hungry
and Mom's earrings jump.
She heats tortillas over the flames
and balances a plate of eggs
dancing in the hot grease.
All the time
a beer bubbles in Dad's hand
while he eyes everyone.
"Shouldn't eat alone, not right,"
he says, "Hurry up."
And I begin grace
for the second time this night.
I glance at Mom who hides
her hands behind her apron,
moving them as if she's going
to roll her apron into a ball.
After he's finished, he drinks more.
I study the field next door.
Mom hates the field and the foxtails
that dig and hide in my socks.
Behind her clotheslines
she curses the field and the drifters
who come and start their campfires,

then wrap themselves with newspapers
before falling asleep.
I trace their shadows
and the leaping flames on nights
when the glass fogs up.
I make up stories about them
with no pain or anger.
Then Dad pounds for another beer.
I move, thinking about our dog
when he circles his pole
and tightens his chain,
knotting it up.
How he tries to leap,
snapping at himself.

CRAYONS

Coco, my youngest aunt, dropped her fan,
sat behind her father's store counter,
sifted through the rice pail, bored,
then studied my crayon drawings,
their smooth textures and warned me
not to stare at a pissing dog
because I would go blind—I jumped
from her lap, pretending to fly,
speaking of America, my other home.

Grown up, I returned to Mexico
and stood by my aunt's deathbed.
Her four daughters, half-dressed,
stared at me, the stranger.
I turned from their mother's face,
feeling sickened by the countless flies
living and breeding on the walls.

One girl rattled Coco's pain killers,
the others sprinkled the dirt floor.
Coco had them put on shoes,
warning of worms in the moist soil.
Coco said on the first summer we met
I could draw her face with my crayons;
leaves surrounded her face,
egg-shaped, a squiggle for a mouth,
long bangs and eyes, new buttons.

LABOR

I cut the oleanders
working around the fruit trees.
With a stiff wrist,
I let my arm
and machete do all the work.
Dirt dulls my edge;
I swing,
protecting the blade.
I shape like memory,
leaving what I need to see.
While the trees
begin to vanish
and their branches spread
against the sky,
I clear my childhood garden
with the scent of grass
at my heels.

MY MOTHER'S STORIES

Mother nailed
a cross of palm leaves,
its end yellowing, frayed.

At night Mother said if we noticed it, especially its arms
reaching down to the feet, we would see a woman dressed in
cotton, a whore loosening the ankle strap of her sandal. She
tapped her shoe against a wall and rubbed her sore foot. She
pointed to a street unlike ours where men stomped the ground,
dancing and blowing out fireballs. The feathers around their
heads and waists bounced and flared. The fire breathers danced
around their gas tanks, whirling their torches for the passing
cars. On the corner women with red ribbons woven into their
long braids peeled potatoes, cutting them into thin slices, then
fried them in ash-colored coffee cans. Their children blew into
small plastic bags, then filled them with hot chips and sold them.
A man who also left his town came to play lemon leaves, the way
one plays a blade of grass.

And a slow-paced greyhound sniffed
at the hunger around them.

Before that the cross was an Indian girl who hobbled, helped by
a wooden crutch. She waited for tourists, especially young
couples. Leaning on the crutch, she twisted her leg and held out
her hand for the walkers. Yet when the rain came, she threw the
crutch over her shoulder and ran, skipping over the pools in the
plaza. Her sandals slapped the wet cobbles.

"Please, one more, tell us one more."

Our bed's worn-out springs drew us in the middle, huddled like
flour sacks. Mother read us the Bible and when we were bored

she made up stories. At school Sister Maria asked: "Where did you hear that? Who told those evil lies? Child, I'll not hurt you if you tell me now."

She was also a wife
who braved a smile
while she crossed a muddy river.
She held her skirt up,
wading through the currents
trying not to spill a pot of coffee beans
she had just bought at the market.

Foam glistened on her thighs
and the river soiled her dress.

Mother told us the wife
found herself waiting for a train.
There was war; a revolution started.
Her fellow soldaderas rested,
too tired to speak.
They wore their bandoliers loose,
their shawls tied around their waists,
dragging when they marched.
They leaned on cargo boxes
and on bundles of clothing;
only their hands seemed to move;
the rest was reposed.
As the wife stood,
her rifle was planted
in front of her legs,
both hands grasping it,
elbows slightly out,
the rifle steadying her wait,
her war.

EYES HELD BY A LANDSCAPE

All the framed faces of a bus
stir him on as he passes them,
seeing a cross that marks
where a car went off the cliff.
Someone lit candles for the dead;
someone nailed their photos on.
The signs warning of crossing cows
and the reds of cactus apples blur;
he plunges into a landscape of bees
darting among the lemon blossoms,
reddening fruit near a river
thin under mango leaves.
A girl swims in a muddy pool,
her body already half-stone,
hair caked, wet straw.
She dives back into the earth.
Only a road of valleys that funnels
into a green web stays in sight
as he veers by curves that hug
the faces of cut rocks.
His aunt has already heard
the news of his father's death.
She lives in these mountains
only the Coca-Cola trucks will visit.
Her road is almost washed away
and the TV antenna tied to a pipe
looks homemade, ready to give.
The family dog will bark,
leaping as if to bite,
then go back to his flies again,
asleep on the dust he kicked up.

OFELIA'S DREAM

Roberto returned with a dog-faced
Chevrolet that could cross the river
leading to our mountain town,
and everyone admired him,
especially my father.

During storms when the cliffs litter
our only road with rocks
and the river floods its banks
and crossing it is almost impossible,
Roberto made it through.
Father introduced him to me
like he was a hero.

Once when he was courting me,
we rushed our neighbor to town
because she split her thumb in half
skinning a cactus.
At the plaza a young man
gazed at us, asking where Roberto
had found such a truck.
While Roberto's grin grew,
I shared in his pride.

On the Day of Our Lady
he asked me to ride with him.
Father said: "It's respectable,
soon you will be married."
And I sat as I had
at my father's table
when they had set the date.

People cheered as we drove
the Virgin Mary and her gown of flowers
through streets lined with ribbons.
Once we stopped, Roberto led me
into a crowd moving to the church,
and I turned back,
seeing Mary on a platform
being carried by several men.
Her extended arms balanced her
while she tottered,
her hands floating above the crowd.
The candles surrounding her were lit,
and the rising smoke caged her
and unraveled like long braids.

Last night when the moonlight
filtered through my lace curtains,
lighting my wall with a figure,
I saw Mary's veiled face.
She gestured, whispering my name
as if to tell me a secret,
then she threw off her shawl,
wrapped it around her waist,
impatient and angry with me
for being swept away
and agreeing to marry Roberto,
a decent man I did not love,
but I could not move from my bed.
She floated and was gone,
vowing she would return.

THE LETTERS FROM SCHOOL

Blue is for the troublemakers,
white for the award-winning students
and red for the lice-infested ones.
In spring the nurse inspects and some
lock their jaws waiting in line,
others begin to scratch and giggle
when the nurse holds the comb to light.
A few imagine they hear the "crack,"
the breaking of the louse's clear egg.

By the blackboard a stickman stands
with opened hands and a painted face,
waiting like a cross and his fingers
count the passing school hours.

A girl smudges her penciled-in heart
then folds the paper—it becomes
a bookmark swinging by her side
when the teacher calls her up.
With the bells ringing she runs,
the pinned letter rubbing her chin,
blushing through the white envelope.

At home a screen door swings,
its pumping arm brings in the night.
She translates the letter.
A hallway extends into sleep
where she sees another
locking her leg on a crossbar,
flipping, and the sand in her shoes
streams off in waves, then she stops,

raising her hand, showing her bracelet,
a tied string to ward off cooties.

The clicking of her heels
is like the calling of her name.
While she counts the empty seats,
a wooden man opens his arms.
The bookmark hides in its story.

FLORA'S PLEA TO MARY

I have kissed your son's feet,
blood stained, cold as porcelain
and you bless me from your window,
a patchwork of colors warming me.
I lit a candle, watched its dance,
then prayed into my cupped hands.
Your sorrow of losing your only son
strengthens me now, so hear me.
I spilled hot water on my husband's lap.
He cursed, pulled my hair, kicking me;
I can't taste the salt of my lips.
Everything on my plate is the same.
At home my husband opens our door
as if I knocked, searching for me,
expecting me to be hiding in the yard.
I know what I must do while he waits.
When he falls asleep drunk with hate,
I will steal my children back and hide.
Until then, pain and what is not
is all the same to me—my anguish
is enough to bring you my prayers.

STYROFOAM BOATS

From a window Mother pointed
at the cloud's darkness,
warning of another downpour.
I tied a string to my boat;
the current did the rest.

The leaves and mud soiled
the yellow blur I raced.
The string snapped: my boat
plunged with the rest.
I jumped in to search.

Tip-toed, Mother leaned,
gazing at the large drain.
She pressed her cheek white,
fogging the glass blind.

I heard her tap the glass,
calling me back inside
while I knelt by the drain,
feeling its mouth pull.

TELLING SISTER MY NIGHTMARE

Not being careful enough I didn't
decline the cup of lemongrass
the evil couple offered me.
They wanted to drug me,
then abuse me—You know: the man
while his old maid watched.
The grassy blades were so neat,
so tightly knotted that I stirred,
cooling my sip. My breath flowed out.
I sank in my chair, watching my tea darken,
then the floor rushed, the rug's roses flamed.
I fell and dug my nails into the rug.
I tried to get up, but the photos on the wall
laughed at me. The evil couple's feet
moved towards the tea soiling the rug,
towards me. I was drowning. Air bubbles
rushed by, blanketing me. I looked up
and their hands plunged into the water
reaching for me. I couldn't swim,
falling into seaweed—it danced around me.
My nostrils and lungs burned.
I tried planting my feet,
pushing up to the closing light,
but I couldn't find the ground,
only the vines entangling me.

FACES IN BLOOM

When we are old we will have them.
Wallets will be full of them
and we will hold them up
so that our faces can see.

POOR HAROLD'S LUCK

On Tuesday morning
Harold fell from a ladder
and broke his hip
while picking lemons in his backyard.
The ladies of the block
thought he was a gentleman
when he'd turn his sprinklers off
letting them pass
with their sniffing dogs.
The kids said he was cranky
most of the time
and the Mexican claimed
that Harold would not shake hands
the first time they met.
At the end Harold was fond
only of doing his yard
even when he walked with a cane.
All morning Harold had been down
and the sun made his cane
too hot to touch.
His leg was stiff with pain.
He listened for a breeze,
for his chimes to ring.
He wanted to refill a feeder
for the hummingbirds that hover
and sip the red sugar water
before darting into evening.
And under his lemon tree
Harold cursed his luck.
The kids who teased and unnerved him
were still at school.

They liked to cat-walk across his wall
and when Harold heard them,
he'd press his face against his window,
wielding his cane.
He had yelled for too long.
He stopped wondering if he could
flag down a passing car out front.
He looked for his cane,
wondered about his wife
and said: "Where is it? How dumb,
how dumb to fall,
how maddening and my wife
at school taking her painting class,
just think of that, at her age
painting those silly sunflowers
and her always asking me what I think.
And she brought it up again,
mentioned how nice a lawn service
would be, how easy it would be.
She knows I can't stand those shits
and their noisy blowers that fan
the trash down the street.
They always cut the grass too short,
weakening the poor roots,
inviting dandelions to thrive.
Then they roam, yellowing the lawn
with their poison sprayers that leave
an odor of rotten fruit, overly sweet,
unnatural as their dark chemicals.
Shit on them all. Once I'm better,
I'll do my own work again."

WINTER FRUIT

At dusk, the sun-bleached fence
shades pomegranates splitting their peel,
open to the birds,
cracking and gaping, jaws.
Some shrink in the ivy.
Moss greens their seeds.

I recall my system: First,
I put on rubber gloves
and with a wooden hammer I tap,
opening it, letting its seeds
roll and bleed on the plate.

The pomegranates ripen,
the faces of winter, the stories
of their leafless branches.
They are death's charm bracelet.

Once I sat next to them
sunning myself, letting the light
warm my closed eyes.
Their stone faces let me dream.

I saw their faces:
the bicycle boy who did not
see the car pulling out,
the housewife who was shocked
by the glaring eyes
and the policeman who aimed his flashlight
at the waiting shadow.

At night I imagine their faces
suspended on a Ferris wheel
that sweeps out the darkness
with its whirling lights.
Some figures grip the bars.
At the top lovers kiss.
Two girls throw their arms up,
screaming at the rushing ground.

THE LAME BOY RETURNS

My smile mocked your speed—
your nicknames dragging behind.
I can't recall your name.
Has it been that long?

You bobbed and planted your crutch,
a recarved bedpost, stumping a trail.
Your other hand balanced your stride,
and waved, but I ran to my friends,
your leg a symbol of our health.
You heard our jokes and still played along,
chasing our laughter through the street,
finding me in a circle of flaring faces,
planning to run even faster from you.

Your leg did not fade
like a childhood fear,
like the creaking of my dark house.
Your limp is more than flesh,
casting a larger shadow now.

FIRST ILLNESS

He does not recall how sick he was,
just a moist towel over his eyes,
a fever burning, a dream of clowns
squirming under a trapeze artist
pedaling a unicycle—his cautious
wheel sank, moving down the rope.
His balancing pole cut wobbly circles
that rose in the tent's smoky air.
A nervous sigh from his watchers
made him glance back at the world
and notice the worry in their faces.

THE PHONE BOOTH AT THE CORNER

At sixty Grandfather
stayed the whole summer.
New to America and to us,
he kept to himself at first.

After a week, he asked me
about our neighborhood bar
and so we went—that day
mother put him under my care.
We walked by a phone booth.

The phone began to ring.
A parrot whistled from a porch.
Grandfather pushed the door.

Grandfather spoke only Spanish,
so he couldn't reply.
The door, divided by hinges,
opened by pulling a handle
but Grandfather pushed.

I leaned, trying to push.
His fear of being trapped
grew with his effort, pale
like the palms I faced.
The door folded when he gave up
and he began to laugh with me.
The bird sang and all of us
broke the air with our voices.

FLAVIO'S NEW HOME

Luz, Colton is not a big city or nice,
nor does it have a park where lovers kiss
as we did in Chula's backyard
the night I told you I was leaving Tijuana.
You will not find a lit fountain,
let alone a decent plaza where people can just be,
but this place has a great freeway
that laces through it, bringing cities closer.
How the freeway's ivy clings
and when I am thinking of you,
I am drawn to the fast lane,
the way it curls, spirals and bridges,
always leading back to itself
like a sacred serpent swallowing its tail.
All the way the arrows and green signs,
fluorescent, assure me of name and mile.
Luz, how easily you forget me here.
I am still your Flavio, the Flavio
who, when I couldn't use my brother's car,
rode his ten-speed through the dangerous shoe district
just to see you and who waited
until you flicked your porch light off and on,
the sign your parents were asleep
and once together we never wasted time.
Now I have a job repairing flat tires.
Cash in my money order and come to Colton.
Sometimes, closing the door of my pick-up,
I imagine you beside me,
digging through your purse, looking around us.
You find your lipstick, pushing it up,
then tilt my mirror to your lips,

telling me of your hunger, unsure
if you want to eat at the open market,
or at your uncle's stand,
but like always you promise yourself
a fruit juice with crushed ice
and sprinkled brown sugar.

I WAS NOT SURE

I was not sure I was alive
under last night's slender stars.
I was not sure that was my voice,
or if my words were waves pushing
your fears away—I don't know
if that was me who touched you.
Were my fingers wild as soldiers?
Was that me and my green army?

BY LOOKING AT MY FURNITURE

I ease into my past, a cushion
or even the duct-taped arms
of my spring rocker calm me.

We must move, again.
I have already sold a chair,
bicycle, two tube radios,
the junk I can part with.

All morning you folded clothing
and paced, searching for your keys.
You were mad at me
for not finding small boxes,
for not labeling the ones we have.

In an overfilled closet
you found your shoe box of buttons:
some were going to adorn vests,
or maybe go into making a necklace
or even some crazy earrings.

You rattled the box,
clearing your mind of those years
you junked at thrift stores.
You are not ready to move.
I mean we are not.

RECOMMITTED

1.

At the mental ward I chew
a button on my sleeve, looking off.
My doctor—I know what he's thinking.
I chew at the check-in counter,
rehearsing what I will say:
"Tell me again, I must give away
my rights. I want to hear why
you need for me to sign."
I walk through the security doors
knowing that later in my room,
in my sleeping ear a promise
will turn to poison, a pill
white as the button I mouth.

2.

My wife doesn't blame me
because I tell her the paint
I used at the body shop
hardened in my brains as well.

Usually, she's the first to cut
the plastic wristband labeling me
when I am released from this ward.

Behind her clothesline, she slaps
her wet hips and blames my pills
for my inability to get it up.
I sprayed cars for too long.
She doesn't turn from my body
but she holds me, guiding my face,
pressing her breasts, arching back,
asking me to fall to my knees.

3.

During our healing session,
I tap my foot and scratch my scalp.
A pill bundles all my nerves
wrapping, rolling me away.
I think of not thinking,
of working for a living,
of a yellow bulldozer
I drove as a young man.
I cleared an orange grove
of all the stumps and roots,
of all the roots worming out
of the soil like snakes.
I keep myself busy,
feeling the steering sticks
shake my hands, my body,
dulling my grip.

4.

I taste the sweat of my mouth,
crossing myself the way I was taught.
I want to rise out of this bed,
and comb my wife's hair,
smelling her shampoo.
I want to smell that odor
of a working man
and remind myself who I was.
The keepers of my sanity
bring me wax cups of water.
Outside my room they pace,
holding their writing boards,
checking me off with their pens,
but I am tired of them, tired
of the questions I must avoid,
of nods I make like a confessor.
I need only my wife,
like she is this hour,
asleep on her side of our bed.
I will curl up by her side
and listen to her breathing,
easing into her dream.

WHEN YOU LEAVE

Carry pride in your fist,
                walk,
        stop only to check the time,
know the corner store,
              turn and smile back,
      whistling past the barking dog.

Sit at a bar stool,
       never too warm,
               never
     be the first to talk
     of politics or sports.

When listening to a lady
       never rattle
your change, unless
       she's doing you,
doing you the business first.
     Be always willing
     not to lead.

Nod even if you disagree,
           listen,
     pretending is an art.

Never repeat this,
      especially to lovers who seek
      your advice on matters.

Wear your eyes in shade,
          rest under dreamy suns,
          and sing if you have to,
          fall in love if you have to,
          but only to the day's motion,
simply silent and in transition, always.

Juan Delgado
is an associate professor of English
at California State University, San Bernardino.

THE CONTEMPORARY POETRY SERIES

EDITED BY PAUL ZIMMER

THE CONTEMPORARY POETRY SERIES

EDITED BY BIN RAMKE